John,

Enjoy this book with our love,

Mom & Dad Strouse

Song of a Soul Set Free

# Song of a Soul Set Free

## Celebrating Life in the Spirit

by
Caroline Gilroy

Beacon Hill Press of Kansas City
Kansas City, Missouri

Permission to quote from the following copyrighted versions of the
Scriptures is acknowledged with appreciation:

*The Holy Bible, New International Version* (NIV), copyright ©
1973, 1978, 1984 by the International Bible Society.

The *Revised Standard Version of the Bible* (RSV), copyrighted
1946, 1952, © 1971, 1973.

*The Living Bible* (TLB), © 1971 by Tyndale House Publishers,
Wheaton, Ill.

10  9  8  7  6  5  4  3  2  1

These pages are lovingly dedicated
to the man who has allowed me
to call him "Dad,"
and to the woman who has become
my spiritual mother . . .
Dr. and Mrs. A. F. Harper

# Contents

# Contents

# Foreword

Christian autobiography is both personal testimony and authentic Christian witness. It is one of the best tools for Christian teaching, and a powerful instrument for spreading the gospel.

*Song of a Soul Set Free* is candid Christian witness. In it Caroline tells of her journey into the experience of entire sanctification. She also records her experience and her reflections over a six-month period after she had been filled with the Holy Spirit. Here is clear witness to the search, the finding, and some early experiences of life in the Spirit.

Most of these reflections were recorded day by day during six months of life in a Nazarene parsonage. They were organized under chapter headings in order to show more clearly the various ministries of the Holy Spirit as we grow and mature in the sanctified life. After the first chapter, the meditations have been arranged in the original day-by-day format to reflect accurately the way Christian growth occurs. The newly sanctified reader will here discover many parallels to his own experiences.

These messages will have a special appeal to all who seek to follow Christ in a family setting—wives, mothers, and fathers. Here you will also find clearly reflected many experiences unique to parsonage families and to Sunday School teachers.

The Gilroy family includes their three children, whom you will meet—Tabitha, Layton, and Charity. During this first year of walking in the Spirit, two foster children were also part of the family. Jan and Arron are Indian brothers, wards of the Canadian courts, who were given a Christian home by the Gilroys.

Paul prayed that his Christian friends "might be filled

with all the fulness of God" (Eph. 3:19). That is our prayer for every reader who has not yet been sanctified wholly. We would like you also to be able to sing the *Song of a Soul Set Free*. For every sanctified follower of Christ, we pray that you may "grow in grace, and in the knowledge of our Lord and Saviour Jesus Christ" (2 Pet. 3:18).

—A. F. HARPER

# Preface

## That Our Children Will Know

"Ye shall receive power, after that the Holy Ghost is come upon you: and ye shall be witnesses unto me" (Acts 1:8).

Walter was preaching an up-to-par sermon on holiness. As he spoke, I recalled a legend read in earlier years.

This legend told about a team of beautiful horses commissioned to leave their lovely green pastures to work in the depths of the West Virginia coal mines. From the day they entered the mine until their deaths, they would never see the glow of sunlight again.

Eventually these horses had a colt. Their favorite family pastime was to tell the colt of the wonderful world they had known outside the pitch-dark mines. These stories planted a desire in the little one's heart to romp in the grassy fields and to feel the sun's warmth on his own back. But the years passed, and the young one never saw any evidence that the wonderful stories his folks had shared with him were true. He died believing that his mother and father had told him nothing but lies.

This sad story is only a myth. But my own children dying in darkness could become a reality.

Oh, how I pray that our children will not simply hear us share tales of the wonderful experience of entire sanctification, but that through our lives, they will feel the flow of the Holy Spirit in their own souls.

I pray that my husband, along with holiness ministers around the world, will preach the message continuously and clearly; that all of us laymen and laywomen in the church

11

will find the experience and live holy lives; and that our children and their children will know that God's call to holy living is an experience, not just an idealistic fable.

"Lord, help me to live a daily life yielded to the Holy Spirit so that others may see the living reality of the truths they have heard."

# 1

## My Journey into High Country

# The Conscious Beginning

Where does one begin to tell about her richest, sweetest, yet most agonizing journey? To tell about the nightmares faced in the gloomiest streets traveled might cause her readers to fear. To tell about the brightest dreams might cause them to sneer, "Impossible."

So where to begin?

Perhaps the logical place to begin this story would be at the place where my journey took on conscious reality—a nondescript conference room of ACTC (Atlantic Christian Training Center) in Tatamagouche, N.S. For it was in the confines of those barren chambers that our district superintendent dragged out his trusty tape recorder along with a lengthy tape for the evening devotions for our fall pastors' and wives' retreat.

It was hard to imagine what this secondhand sermon preached by a founding father of years gone by could possibly have to say to me, and so I prepared to spend the minutes ahead daydreaming. Yet as much as I tried to tune him out, I could not. His message concerning broken covenants tugged at my heart. Before the closing prayer, I had renewed a promise made to God one week before our wedding.

The pastor had challenged our congregation to join him in reading *10 chapters a day from the Bible.* Perhaps a week before one's wedding is not a good time to make promises to anyone, let alone to God; but it was done. I signed the contract and took up the task. Have you ever noticed how long some of the chapters are in the Gospels or in Exodus or Chronicles? I had almost signed away my entire future.

But I kept that promise faithfully—until about the second year of our marriage. Church activities were picking up, Tabitha was born, and life became more demanding. It was about then that I began to lose contact with our Heavenly Father as well. Other things were put first in my life; God just didn't fit in. I was too busy being a pastor's wife to be a Christian.

But at that retreat, listening to a secondhand sermon, I faced the grave state of my soul. Once again I determined to pick up my used-only-on-Sunday Bible and started plowing through those chapters.

Perhaps 10 chapters a day from God's Word is extreme, though I am not finding that true. Extreme or not, I am thankful for a God-inspired pastor who led me to such a deep commitment. My gratitude knows no limit for that saintly founding father who preached a sermon decades before my time. He encouraged me to keep my covenant with God. I am even a bit thankful for Rev. Bahan and his trusty tape recorder.

Upon looking into the Word of God, something wonderful began to happen. Whether reading in the Old or the New Testament, God met me and showed clearly the deep need of my carnal heart. Then began a hunger and thirst after righteousness. Yet the more I read from the Holy Scriptures, the more I realized my soul was engulfed by repulsive, frightening darkness.

My devotion to Christ came in spurts; the reality of His presence came in spurts. I was never certain if I was for Him or against Him. There was always doubt as to whether I was going to serve Him or deny Him. I limped along in the Christian life, sensing there was more, hoping and praying there was more, but never quite believing there was more for me. My soul longed for sanctification, love from a pure heart, but my mind denied it as a possibility for the wretched state of my heart.

My soul was dying in the blackness that surrounded it. Often I would catch rays of the promised light reflected from

16

high country, but I never was so wrapped in it that my heart could relax from the strain of trying to see in the dark.

Christ continued to plead, "Be ye holy," and I continued to respond, "If only I could."

## Sidetracked

My soul trudged on in torturous steps. The longing to surrender all to the One who deserves our utmost affection pounded out the heartbeats in the onward struggle.

But at times when the blessed land seemed just around the bend, there were detours to slow down progress. It seemed I would never see the promised heights.

My unsanctified heart met with such a detour the spring Walter's clerical credentials were to be transferred into the Church of the Nazarene from the United Church of Canada. For it was then, at our district assembly in Summerside, P.E.I., that my well-trained hidden nature surfaced.

This ordination service was to be a very special affair for our family. We had looked forward to it for months. The patterns for the white dresses for Tabitha, Charity, and me had been selected with care. Layton and Walt were going to wear white slacks and navy blazers to match. Everything was going to be perfect.

But I hadn't taken unusually hot weather into consideration when planning for our perfect celebration, and hadn't prepared for grumpy kids or a totally exhausted body. Nor had there been room made for receiving the message Walt was to relay when he returned to our lodging after the day's business session had been completed.

My peace-loving husband approached the subject cautiously, but that didn't help. I was in no mood for the discussion. Some ladies on the district had expressed their concern to the D.S. about my manner of dress. The fight was on.

I dared not lose and let the opposition win. Deep down I wanted to submit, to consider their feelings in love, to say, "It doesn't matter anyway." But I couldn't; there just wasn't the love it would take.

That evening, I entered the sanctuary of the Summerside Church of the Nazarene, proudly looking my grandest— rebellious heart and all.

## A New Sense of Direction

Perhaps it's the challenge presented. Perhaps it's the stubborn streak inherited from Mom. But more than likely, it is simply my poor sense of direction that proves almost every "You can't miss it" prophecy to be a sad and very obvious mistake. For I can miss it. No matter how good, how complete, how simple the instructions given, I can miss it without any effort at all.

And even though the best instructions had been given for the route to follow on this journey, it seemed my soul would be forever searching blindly for the destination in the travel onward. There had been guidance by the best road signs in excellent Sunday School classes. Numbers of dedicated teachers pointed in the right direction. Superior pastors and evangelists had slated the course through their clear gospel messages. But the road stretched ever so darkly before me.

Licking wounds inflicted by well-meaning friends, my soul was torn between what it longed to be and what it was. I was either earth's sweetest mother and wife or earth's poorest excuse for a lady. I was either forgiving and bighearted or grudging and petty.

Yet the desire to be constantly loving was always my companion. When by extra effort on a sunny day I managed to be what was desired, my companion proudly acknowledged the achievement. On the more typical, don't-touch-me days, I was haunted by failure.

The roadsides marked the path clearly for the soul's climb; but it's easy to lose one's way, even on a well-marked path, when one is traveling in bitter darkness.

And then I heard the words. Whether they had been heard before, they sounded forth as a bell pealing through the night to guide sojourners home. The camp evangelist had offered that day's road map and asked that we close with the melodious prayer, "Oh, to be like Thee! Oh, to be like Thee."

As the words echoed through the aluminum sanctuary, they also whispered through the corridors of my weary mind. I realized that the words of that song were beautifully defining the inner desire of heart. The longing ever growing in my soul was to be sweet, gentle, loving, patient—all that our Savior personified—and to be that consistently.

My heart surely beat my feet to the altar of prayer that morning. In that moment, via those words, my soul was given a new sense of direction. Oh, how I wanted to be like Jesus.

But as Mel McCullough, Dr. Harper, Walt, and the D.S. gathered around to encourage on the journey, I realized progress would not be made. I was too aware of those who had gathered around. As usual I was satisfied by all the special attention being given. No longer was the weight of the carnal nature so crushing. Rather, it was pleased that so many had come to pray.

Prayers went up, and everyone went to lunch.

Yet those words, those precious, haunting words followed. The question was, Could I become like Jesus? Was that image of His perfect love available? Could I ever be sanctified wholly? Would I ever see high country? Or was I, as some had suggested, expecting too much from God?

# Unsolicited Guidance

Our final family camp in the Maritimes was a meaningful one for us. During that week, we had the opportunity to say our farewells to many of our district friends. Also during that week we had been able to grow a friendship with Dr. and Mrs. Harper.

Throughout this Big Lake experience Walter and I observed the Harpers with a dawning awareness of their qualities. We were impressed by their gentle warmth and genuine interest in the campers. We were deeply moved by their humble, unobtrusive spirits. They spent time just listening to our dreams and plans for our new congregation in Calgary, Alta. They laughed at our silly jokes, smiled at our immaturity, and endured our chatter.

It wasn't easy to say good-bye to our new friends when that camp's final hymn had been sung and the final prayer had been offered. One week of sharing is far too short a time for love to be satisfied. Yet reluctant good-byes were said with an unspoken wish that someday we would meet again.

But I was not prepared for that reunion of spirits to be so soon, nor had I expected it via the postal system. Within a week a letter addressed to me was delivered to our chaotic, nearly packed-up house. It was signed "Albert Harper."

Mixed emotions stirred in my soul while reading his words. I didn't need or want his advice. I could make it the rest of the way quite well on my own, thank you.

And yet he felt he should write the letter. As the frustrations quieted, I became grateful for this person who would open his heart in such a way. It was gratifying that he had stuck out his neck to try to help.

After all that day's packing was done, and Walt and the kids were tucked into bed, I sat in the middle of our soon-to-be-left family room to respond to the letter.

I admitted having been wrestling with the issue he had discussed. I just couldn't conform to the wishes of the church simply because it was the church or because of being a pastor's wife.

My soul was crumpled while trying to empty my thoughts on the page. I was hurt and angry, ready to quit.

His reply came before we left for our new life in the West. The major problem with all his unsolicited guidance was that the Lord had spoken to me, and I was becoming bitter.

Surely the road would be smoother 3,000 miles away.

## Distance Makes No Difference

The reminder soon came that one just can't say good-bye to God. Our Heavenly Father refuses to be dumped by the roadside. He will not permit His children to leave Him behind as they explore new territories.

Our move west went well, considering it was made with three small children and a rascally schnauzer. Our cherished antiques survived the packing, jostling, and unpacking without a scratch. The adjustments from life in a small Eastern town to life in a progressive Western city were made easily. The lure of bright lights, bustling malls, and sophisticated entertainment had always been appealing.

But it seemed I would never adjust to living in our church-attached parsonage. Something inside refused to accept the quarters provided. All the hopes and dreams of having a perfect home and building an ideal family were being crushed by the resentment building up in my soul.

My steps seemed more and more sluggish in the journey. My soul was more distressed than ever before as our Heavenly Father kept the hope of high country in my heart, insisting there could be happiness right here if I would just let Him lift the carnal load.

The fact that none of our new parishioners or acquaintances seemed the least bit concerned about my lack of Christian simplicity lessened the burden for a short season. But this relief was temporary. For even though no one else mentioned it, the Lord continued to speak; and I had to face reality. God had not stayed behind. His presence was as much a fact in Calgary, Alta., as it had been in Truro, N.S.

The 3,000 miles distance had made no difference. He was walking with me, loving, understanding, and calling me to absolute surrender to His will—holiness.

## At the Crossroads

Rebellion slowed my steps drastically as I wallowed in the degrading luxury of itemized self-pity sessions. Tasteless portions of our parsonage existence were blown out of proportion, and vision was limited due to tears of bitterness.

Instead of enjoying the family as I longed to enjoy them, I wasted hours and days wishing for a life that wasn't mine. Instead of becoming the Spirit-filled helpmate I wanted and intended to be, I made my husband's job more difficult. Instead of reaching out to lost, hurting souls, I felt someone should be ministering to me. Everything centered around me—what I wanted, what I thought, what I needed.

It was easy to despise the journey more with each step. Deep in my heart was the longing to take a different route. I wanted to travel upward and to help others while so doing. I tried to change course by thinking positive thoughts, pretty thoughts; but there wasn't the inner strength to make the climb. And I didn't want to be led through the valley of the shadow of death to inbred sin.

Finally my soul arrived at the crossroads that demanded response from Walt as well as myself. Either he would have to leave the ministry, or I would have to leave him.

The very thought of life without Walt and the kids was sickening. Yet the thought of a dismal future working for the church, having life regulated by that institution, was even more sickening. There was no other way for us—for *me*—to be happy.

Walt's love for and faith in his Heavenly Father had never failed him; and, thankfully, it did not fail him when we came to the crossroads. My loving husband was confused by my behavior, but he patiently prayed for me. He agreed to leave the pastorate for other full-time Christian service, but he was not willing to stop ministering.

With this promise from Walt, life looked brighter and the path appeared straighter. Surely the road would be easier to travel as a layperson.

No, this new walk would not lead to high country, but it looked like it would lead to greener pastures for our entire family.

## The Uphill Climb

Fears that perhaps Walt shouldn't leave the ministry, that perhaps God had given him a call to walk this path (and me with him) could not be set aside. Even though in daydreams life was blissful as a "normal" person, doubts began to arise that we could ever be rid of the pastorate as more and more time escaped from us.

These fears and dreams caused me to anticipate, with mixed emotions, Dr. and Mrs. Harper's upcoming visit to conduct the 10-day fall revival services. I suggested to Walt that perhaps, out of respect for these dear people, I should dress more simply.

The coming of our honored guests stirred our hearts, our home, and our little congregation. Throughout the week, Dr. Harper ministered to us in the simple beauty of holiness.

Mrs. Harper shared with me as we scrubbed what seemed to be endless piles of dishes. And no one even so much as mentioned the word *worldliness*.

As the week wore on, I began to wonder if our friends cared about my soul after all. I wanted them to care—not to nag, but to care.

Saturday afternoon I shared with Dr. Harper my desire for Walt to leave the ministry. His unruffled, seemingly apathetic "I see" didn't soothe my aching heart. I wanted him to caution, sympathize, or even lecture, but not to sit placidly in that straight-backed Victorian parlor chair saying, "I see." At that time I was convinced our chat had been a total waste of emotional energy.

But now it is clear that the dilemma was carried directly to the Lord by someone who cared more than was evident. The Harpers were praying. And prayer was what my soul desperately needed at that point.

Sunday afternoon the house was filled with silence, everyone sleeping soundly; but the pounding of my heart seemed almost deafening as I began the uphill climb, seeking God's best.

No one seemed to notice that the struggle continued through the Sunday evening service. As the congregation was being dismissed, I left the sanctuary. Sitting in the quiet darkness of our living room, I wept agonizing tears. The revival was over, tomorrow the Harpers would leave our home, and my soul was not in. The cloudy fear I had known prior to their arrival was not that we would have an encounter; but instead, the fear was that I would not have an encounter with God.

After a brief time of fellowship, the Harpers were about to excuse themselves for the night; but my hoarse, strained voice interrupted them by asking Dr. Harper to pray with me in the living room.

I tried to share where I was with this man of God, and he prayed. Then he prayed again and he prayed again.

"Caroline, you pray," he insisted; but the words wouldn't come. "It concerns me that you can't pray," Dr. Harper whispered. It concerned me too.

The pains of becoming beautiful in holiness were real that night, for I was afraid that the Lord would insist that I become a forsaken plain Jane. But He opened my eyes to the possibility of a heart fully cleansed by His blood, and that is what I longed for.

When I came to the gate of the Promised Land, I was more aware than ever that those who had criticized in the past concerning the unyielded area they felt was hindering entrance into high country, could point their finger and cry, "We told you so," if I was to be obedient to the voice of the Savior. Selfish pride was repulsed by the thought of such humiliation.

But the last claim to the right to myself crumbled. Once again in the dim light of God's growing presence it was becoming clear that any price would be worth it, just to be totally His. However, unbelief retarded my progress.

Finally I stammered, "Dr. Harper, what if I give God everything and He doesn't give me a pure heart? What if He doesn't sanctify me wholly?" The revivalist offered some promises to my melting heart and continued to pray.

In becoming willing to be obedient to the Lord, whether He moved in my heart as was expected or not, I yielded to Him on the point He was dealing with me. At that moment the Lord granted just enough faith to step into high country. The conflict was over. By the grace of God, I was in.

## The Comforter Has Come

The autumn Monday morning sunshine broke through, fresh and clean. Even though feeling numb, I knew a battle had been won, emptying of selfishness. The Holy Spirit had cleansed my heart. Yet I had not experienced His fullness.

The night before, I had sincerely given God everything. And it was becoming more and more clear concerning His promise that if I would tarry, the Comforter would come.

Early one evening I prayed by our bed, "Lord, I've come to settle this once and for all. I believe Your Word; You have cleansed my heart, because You said You would. If You will check me when I am tempted to be unchristlike, I will be obedient to Your voice from this day on. Please baptize my soul in love from Your blessed Holy Spirit."

The covenant was sealed. Our Father had heard my request. Almost breathlessly I waited for His visit. It seemed He would not come, although His promise was definite. But then, in the stillness of our room, I could almost hear His footsteps. Ever so gently He entered. The Comforter has come.

## Journeying in High Country

And now almost 20 months later I can say, what a joy to walk with Jesus ... to have Him to guide moment by moment in the travel toward eternity.

The outward circumstances have not changed. We are living in the same church-attached apartment in the same city with the same annoyances; but life has changed within, and truly there is joy—deep, unlimited joy in the Lord that can't be regulated by outward circumstances.

The Holy Spirit not only met my requests, but He also excelled my greatest expectation. He released my spirit.

Since that night months ago, I have known the peace of full surrender. Moments of distress have come, but they have been given to Him. Agonizing moments of being misunderstood have come, but He lifts the burden. Revealed failures have shredded my devoted heart, but He understands my humanness far better than I do. There is a new song of glorious freedom in following Him.

Thankfully, the Lord did not give up. He desired to provide the refreshing touch my spirit craved. He took me to the depths of misery so I could be prepared to learn lessons about His perfect love.

The victory was won in my heart, not in my outward appearance. Just as the Lord dealt with the rich young ruler at his point of rebellious self-centeredness and with Saul of Tarsus at his, He dealt with me at mine. How I praise His name that He did.

# 2

# Reflections on the Search

# Blind: Even with 20-20 Vision

It really is surprising just how blind a person with 20-20 vision can be at times! Though standing looking directly at the letter being sought, I still couldn't see it! It's not clear how long I had been seeking for it, but it was longer than it needed to be.

As a young adult I realized the great need for a Savior. Although my life seemed together, it was apart. The longing in my empty soul could not be ignored.

And He came. Jesus came into my heart and forgave the many foolish and sinful acts. I was in His presence but still couldn't truly see Him. He was within reach, but I didn't possess His sweet spirit.

I spent years searching for the experience that would give full release from the double-minded sin in the heart. I searched the Scriptures, and they left me craving more. I searched at revival services and camp meetings. In the presence of all this glory, I still could not see.

And then, having asked the Holy Spirit to remove the blindness of soul, I was given light. The sight was not pleasant. It revealed a sinful nature pulling me from the One I longed to serve but couldn't. The rotten attitudes were seen that cluttered the heart that needed to be clean. Selfishness was there that clogged the spirit, from which I wanted to be free to become His best.

But as my eyes began to clearly see these barriers, I became open to the Holy Spirit's work, and finally my soul received 20-20 vision. I can see beyond myself now. I can see His face, and His reflection is slowly becoming mine.

Physical blindness is undoubtedly torturous in a world containing so much beauty. But the blindness that almost drained my spirit of every beautiful plan God has for my life, is far more pathetic. My soul can now thankfully sing with the numbers who have gone before, "I once . . . was blind, but now I see" . . . because of His amazing grace!

# Blessed Assurance

I spent time this afternoon on my knees—picking pine needles out of the rug.

We don't use artificial branches and flowers for decorating. We prefer the real thing. Yet at times like today, after struggling to clear those prickly things from our rug, I realize the real thing takes a bit more effort to maintain and to clean up. But there are rewards. This afternoon, while trying to rid the worn, braided carpet of sticky evergreen pieces, I recalled how surprised Mrs. Broadland had been last week as she reached out to test them. "Just wanted to see if they were artificial," she had said with a smile.

I had tried to claim the experience of entire sanctification without paying the price. But this artificial claim led into deep frustration and miserable torture.

Then tenderly the Holy Spirit revealed the vile sin in my heart. He gently but firmly led me to the brink of a genuine cleansing. I held back because of not believing that He would do the work I craved. It was frightening to think of being left in the desert to die. I longed to be His lady, but was afraid of being stripped down to the real person within. It was so much easier to pretend to have a pure heart than to become a living sacrifice. But this way of a divided heart was a torment for me and for our family.

Finally the desire to be like Jesus Christ became such a part of me that the artificial flowers scattered throughout my being could no longer satisfy my hungry heart. Tearfully I begged the Holy Spirit for His touch. I had only one goal, and that was to be entirely His.

The leaves of the new life in my soul today are real. They can stand the test of a curious world. They have wrapped my soul in absolute beauty, and I no longer fear the Savior's presence in my deepest thoughts.

I am ever so thankful the Holy Spirit would not tolerate artificial grace in my heart. I like the real thing so much better.

> *It's real, it's real.*
> *Oh, I know it's real.*
> *Praise God, the doubts are settled,*
> *For I know, I know it's real!*
>
> —H. L. Cox

# No Substitutes, Please!

"Present your bodies a living sacrifice, holy, acceptable unto God, which is your reasonable service" (Rom. 12:1).

Audrey had asked Frank for an opal ring. He gave her a ruby. He was able to give her the gift she had requested; it was available in local shops, and he had the money. But he wanted to give his wife what he wanted to give her. She laughed as she told us the story, but she indicated she still wanted the opal.

One day Christ tapped me on the shoulder. "I want your love." I gave Him only fragments of my affections.

He went on, "I want your talents." Instead of giving them, I responded, "I don't have any to give."

He pleaded, "I want your whole life presented to Me." I gave Him a little time.

I was determined to give Him my gifts, but I gave what *I* wanted to give. Finally He asked for nothing else.

Soon I was no longer certain of His presence and could not sense His nearness. He was not available for conversation as

He had been. When I asked Him, "Why?" His saddened face reflected the pain caused by my refusal to meet His requests. He replied, "I asked for first place in your heart. In your stubbornness, you gave Me substitutes and excuses."

Because of my self-will, He turned His back until emptiness gripped my soul. The agony of His exit left my heart crying for His return. The longing for His fellowship made me willing to give all that He demanded.

Yet how amazing to discover that whatever I have given to Him, He has blessed and returned to my keeping.

I pray that there shall never again be hesitation to present Christ anything He asks. From the heart I can sing:

> *"All to Jesus I surrender;*
> *All to Him I freely give."*

## Let It Not Be That Outward Adorning

"Whose adorning let it not be that outward adorning of plaiting the hair, and of wearing of gold, or of putting on of apparel" (1 Pet. 3:3).

Some of us have to go through a lot of pain to be beautiful. All women—and some men—who have gone through the torture of getting a permanent know what true agony is.

Like every vain person who has walked on God's earth, I enjoy looking my best. That is why there was such an aversion to looking old-fashioned. At that time my concept of the typical holiness woman fell into the category of "Homeliness is next to holiness." I just had *no* intention of looking any worse than absolutely necessary.

This vanity almost crushed my opportunity to realize perfect peace and freedom. Although for eight years I had longed to be pure, I convinced myself that Christian simplicity was an outdated tradition. Perhaps for some it is. But my refusal to comply with this tradition revealed the rebellious resentment in my heart. I did not want to be shown God's will.

Funny thing. If God had promised, "Now, you may have a pure heart in exchange for your money," I would have laughed and told Him, "Sure thing!" If He had insisted on having time and talents, I could have given them easily. I even could have placed reluctantly my most cherished relationships with Walt and the kids on the altar. But when He got down to the last claim to the rights to myself, I withdrew the sacrifice. I wanted to be adorned as I chose.

But there came a day when I longed for Christlikeness more than life itself. The pains of becoming "beautiful in holiness" were still very real. Finally there came an awareness that all the trinkets in the world would not satisfy the hungering in my soul. When Christ's love became dearer than anything else, His cleansing came, along with His perfect peace.

I still don't have any desire to be anything but the best-looking woman I can be. But it is now so clear that the best-looking me is Christ's image reflected in my spirit.

Still I don't want to look like some Christians; but oh, to look like the daughter our Heavenly Father wants me to be!

## Struggle with Self

Antique furniture is intriguing. One wonders how many babies have been rocked in Walt's Boston rocker. A person could almost see a stern schoolmarm scowling at her bunch of rowdies over our precious desk, or imagine the threads created on our coveted spinning wheel.

Because Walter and I prefer the natural beauty of bare wood, we have spent many hours peeling off layers of paint that previous owners had spent hours brushing on. The process is tedious, but it is worth it when unmarred pine or oak begins to peek through the faded colors.

Then carefully Walt has sanded the surface of each piece until it has become smooth enough to receive some protective lacquer. We cherish the results of our hard labor.

Even though these antiquated pieces are a delight, they are outdated and for the most part have been cast aside by our modern society. I love antiques but never wanted to be one!

That is why I fought so hard against the bidding of the Holy Spirit, being so afraid He would insist I become archaic. There was too much pride to permit that.

Years had been spent adding layer after layer of deceptive "paint." My stained heart was well hidden. I dared not be stripped down to the real person.

But the Savior saw deeper than the camouflage. He saw something beautiful hidden within, and He began to indicate the possibilities of being pure.

Finally, realizing that the plainest woman could be lovely if transformed into His lady, my soul cried out for the touch of the Master. And He came!

Ruthlessly He stripped off the gaudy colors of the outward life and gently sanded until His likeness could be recognized.

As He caresses my heart, He is tenderly applying the lacquer of the grace of the Holy Spirit, and His beauty is becoming mine.

God never intended for us to become discarded antiques; but I would, if that is what He asked!

## Tarry Until

We hadn't seen our friends for over a year. We ached to have them with us, to caress them, to share with them. And now they were coming for a 10-day visit . . . they had promised!

36

We spent two weeks preparing for their arrival because we wanted to offer a spotless house as a token of our love for them. The long-awaited afternoon finally arrived.

They had said they would be here at three o'clock, but three came and went. Even though they were trusted friends, we began to doubt whether the joy of entertaining them in our home would be realized.

Time seemed to stretch endlessly before approaching footsteps announced their presence ... they had come as they said they would. We were glad the house was spotless, ready to receive them. Their company brought unspeakable joy to our hearts.

My soul had been longing for the presence of another Promised Friend. I invited Him to come, but He tarried. His Word revealed I was not prepared for Him because of the self-centered filth corroding the spirit. Desperately I sought cleansing. Layer by layer I was stripped of every selfish claim until the depths of my heart revealed purity.

Emptied of self, my house was vacant without Him. The vigil began as I breathlessly waited for His arrival. It seemed He would never come, although His promise was definite. The process was agonizing, but my heart was clean and prepared for His advent.

As hope almost slipped away, I heard His footsteps. Ever so gently He entered ... the blessed Holy Spirit came! The sweetness of His presence has overwhelmed my raptured soul.

> *The Comforter has come! The Comforter has come!*
> *The Holy Ghost from heav'n, The Father's promise*
> *giv'n!*
> *Oh, spread the tidings 'round, wherever man is*
> *found:*
> *The Comforter has come!*
>
> —FRANK BOTTOME

37

# Everything We're Having

"[I pray] that ye might be filled with all the fulness of God" (Eph. 3:19).

The aroma of hot chocolate was floating through the air as I called out, "Who would like some toast to tide them over until spaghetti time?"

"I dos" rang from every section of the house. Uncertain that I had heard her affirmative cry, Charity came running into the kitchen calling, "I want everything we're having."

It was typical of our chubby Charity. I grinned and assured her she would receive everything. Trustingly, our little clown returned to her play; and my heart exclaimed, "O Holy Spirit, I too want everything we're having."

I long to give our little ones good gifts: to be able to offer them toast and hot chocolate after a winter outing; to be able to bundle them up in warm clothes to protect them from cold, stormy blasts; to make them happy and to keep them healthy.

If I, as an earthly parent, crave all of this for our children, it is certain our Heavenly Father longs to give us much more; and we can come running fearlessly into His presence, shouting, "I want everything we're having—today and always! I want every bit of grace and perfect love available through the blood of Jesus Christ. I don't want ever to be satisfied with less than Your very best for my life. I don't want to miss out on anything You have prepared."

And we can ask Him for all of this in childlike faith, because it is His desire to give us the best. He plans to satisfy our hungering souls!

# 3
## The Joy
## of Finding

# God's Special Gifts

"And I will pray the Father, and he shall give you another Comforter, that he may abide with you for ever" (John 14:16).

When each of our children becomes 16, he or she will receive a special gift from me—an inheritance of sorts. I have saved a meaningful part of my youth for each of them.

My dad was an outstanding salesman. Layton will receive a gold medallion that was presented to my father by his company. For Tabitha I have saved the clock with dancing figurines that my mother gave me. To Charity I will present the watch with four dainty diamonds given to me by my brother Jim on my 16th birthday.

These keepsakes have been set aside for our children because I love them. Since each one bears a unique personality, their inheritance needs to be suited to them. As a parent, I want to give each child more than a gift, to give a part of me—something to keep Mommy in his heart forever.

Our Father has special gifts set aside for us too. Some of His inheritances are peace, joy, and love. These gifts are being applied to my life to fit the personality He breathed into me. Each gift is filling me out, enhancing talents, making me the woman He wants to see.

But our Heavenly Father has given more than gifts; He has given himself in the Holy Spirit. He has provided my heart with an everlasting knowledge of the presence of God. It is glorious to know! Even though He has millions of other children, each one is special enough to Him to receive His Holy Spirit and the gifts just suited to him.

And this Gift is making life much more than endurable. Now I am *free* to enjoy every moment. Every occasion is becoming blessed. The simplest delights are profoundly meaningful, from tucking our little ones into fresh, clean beds, to coasting on the Alberta hills.

Praise God. I am free indeed.

# Continuing Assurance

"Hereby we know that he abideth in us, by the Spirit which he hath given us" (1 John 3:24).

"Nothing between my soul and the Savior . . . There's nothing between."

That truth has been clung to this week. Without that precious knowledge, my soul might have been smothered.

This has been one of those times when life has been more public than private. God's clear voice has been muffled by the chatter of the world. There have been interviews with the kids' teachers, library workdays, hospital visits, missionary meetings, and a special night out with our little "big girls." Every event has added some positive dimension to life, but my soul has longed for quiet moments to be wrapped in God's presence.

A full life does not provide much time for seclusion. And the simple tasks of this world are distracting—if they are permitted to be. They can draw attention from the Father and leave one with doubts.

During the darkest hours when the enemy has tried to convince me that my experience is only history, I have claimed that there is "nothing between my soul and the Savior." All is well; sin has not separated us. His perfect love flows through my spirit, and I am His forever. The enemy can bring doubts, but he cannot bring death.

Even now the Holy Spirit is not apparent to the senses, but He is here, filling with himself. He is continuing to make me fit to meet the tasks that await today and tomorrow.

# 4

# The Joy
# of Learning

# Do It Now

Many precious hours have been wasted dreading. Perhaps that is why the Holy Spirit's tailor-made lessons in this area of life have been so dear. Dread is being rooted out of my soul by the joy of learning to do His perfect will minute by minute.

Ever since I can remember, I have hated getting dressed in the morning. It was not laziness, as I always got straight to work. But putting on clothes would be put off until all else was finished. The anvil weight of that unfinished task was always tormenting.

One morning as we wakened our little ones to the beauty of a new day, the Holy Spirit prompted with "Why don't you dress before breakfast, while the kids are getting dressed?"

There was no good argument. We get up early, and our mornings are rarely hurried. So I got dressed. What a delight it was to turn from the farewells to our schoolbound children with that weight lifted! Never again will I be bound by this chore; I have learned to tackle it before it defeats me.

Many times I have dreaded facing church activities because of not being quite sure where to fit in. In the hours preceding these events, dread would make me almost physically ill.

Since the Holy Spirit has been escorting me through the hours of each day, I have been more open to His tender rebukes. I knew this fearful attitude was not pleasing to Him. Finally I asked for His solution to the problem. His plain answer was: "Pray for that event, and pray for the people who will be there."

What a joy to plan for these occasions now, clearly aware that my role is to love and to be prepared by praying to do so.

Such simple things! To get dressed before breakfast. To

pray for church events. To be ready physically and spiritually for my role all day.

A real regret is that so much time has been sifted from my life, simply because I was not tuned in to His Spirit. But I rejoice that there are no dreaded tasks today. He has helped me to be ready and to be free to enjoy the blessings He has provided during these hours!

## Learning to Pray

As a mother, some of the most exciting moments I can remember are those spent listening to the girls' first words. As they gleefully babbled discernible requests, my maternal heart pitter-pattered until it seemed I was going to explode with pride.

Their guttural noises gradually formed into one-syllable words, then two-syllable words, then three-word sentences. Soon we would be able to communicate on a higher level, to become friends.

All of my born-again life I have wanted to be a prayer warrior, to be able to talk with God in a satisfying way. Nothing sounded so holy as to be able to sit and chat with God for lengthy periods.

But all too soon it became plain that I didn't know how to pray. Any heavenly conversation lasting longer than 10 minutes broke my endurance record. My husband spends morning hours on his knees at the church altar. I nicknamed him "Olympic Pray-er," simply because I could not achieve this goal.

But since my heart has been cleansed and freed to be purely related to the Lord, there has followed learning of expression in talking.

At first, the early-morning time spent with God seemed endless; my soul just mumbled. But I needed those dawning minutes to prepare for His perfect love; so I continued to be in the same place daily, and awkwardly attempted to discuss eternal matters with the Father.

But now as the clock calls me away from His throne, my heart groans within me. Now we have so much to share, to discuss, that there is no longer boredom in His presence. Prayers are going beyond the typical one-syllabled "Bless so-and-sos" to definite sentence requests for the needs of loved ones.

The frustrations of not being able to communicate with our Heavenly Father are becoming memories of infant hours in the faith. The Holy Spirit continues to teach how to talk.

## Spankings Help You Grow

"My son, don't be angry when the Lord punishes you. Don't be discouraged when he has to show you where you are wrong" (Heb. 12:5, TLB).

Breakfast leftovers were scattered about the table as we lingered for a few extra minutes of fellowship. Tabitha was gleefully discussing her upcoming birthday when she asked, "Will I grow on that day?"

Walter and I grinned as we tried to explain that she is growing every day. I added, "Your food makes you grow, the water you drink makes you grow, and the fresh air makes you grow."

"And the spankings make you grow," her daddy teased. Her round, blue eyes sparkled as she responded, "No . . . but they help make you grow up to be good. They make you remember what is bad."

As far as our jubilant whirlwind was concerned, the discussion was closed.

But as she danced to more entertaining activities, I recalled how many times our compassionately stern Heavenly Father has had to spank me, to make me grow up to be good. There was a time of rebellion against His ever-present hand applying painful lessons; but now I can remember what is bad, and the list is long!

For one thing, it is bad to jump into jobs one is not called to do. The destruction that unqualified hands can cause in His kingdom has been proven to me. It hurt, but I remember.

Also, it is bad to intervene in personal problems of others if one has not been guided by the Holy Spirit to do so.

Again, I must love every soul, no matter who that one is. It must be better than confessing, "I am sorry for neglecting you."

And last, I remember that selfishness is never Christlike.

There is still more to be learned. But hopefully He will not have to teach me any one lesson twice. These things He has taught, and spankings help make us grow, but they are not fun.

## "If Any Man Sin"

"My little children, these things write I unto you, that ye sin not. And if any man sin, we have an advocate with the Father, Jesus Christ the righteous" (1 John 2:1).

"I want to love you," Tabitha sobbed.

We had left her to the care of a baby-sitter last night, and she had misbehaved. During the washing of breakfast dishes, she felt exiled.

I stopped to draw our little one near. "Honey, I do love you and will always love you. But I am disappointed. Now you go to your room." Shoulders drooping, Tabitha strolled to her room.

Shortly she returned. "Mommy, I want to pray to ask Jesus to forgive me."

We prayed. And I hugged her and assured her that Jesus had forgiven her and Mommy had forgiven her. It was all over. Our miniseeker radiated with the peace that forgiveness of sins brings.

As she bounced on her way, I prayed that somehow Tabitha would sense the difference between wanting forgiveness simply to feed her selfish desire to be loved, and that of truly being sorry that she had done wrong. I prayed she would come to the Savior for a cleansed spirit always because she is miserably tortured by her sin.

And I remember the minutes spent in the prayer spot earlier this morning.

Last night I had feebly given in to a human whim. In itself the act was not sinful, but it extended into sin.

And this morning I sat before the Savior with drooped shoulders. Oh, how I longed to feel His love, to have Him hug me. Yet there was not a sense of His presence.

"O Jesus," I whimpered, "I am sorry. Please come and love me. I cannot live without Your love."

Silence.

"Jesus," I finally cried, "I sinned last night. I know You forgive me, because You have promised to. Whether feeling Your love or not, I am going to try to serve You. I want to be Yours more than anything else and am determined to never repeat that act again."

In that instant, peace was mine.

In the beginning, I wanted forgiveness to make me feel good. In the end, I craved a cleansing because I was truly sorry for my deed. I was set on never yielding to that temptation again—*never.*

49

# Sharpened Pencils

"Lovest thou me?" (John 21:15).

A half-dozen senior high young people ventured out on this cold, snow-drifted morning to hear my words of wisdom. They were "Getting Acquainted," which was their favorite segment of every lesson.

Inquiries one to four in the section were general questions. One was, "How do you like your teacher?" The Sunday School pupils gave typical replies: "Teachers—ugh!"

But the final queries zeroed in on our devotional lives. There were no avenues of escape. Two or three of the teens squirmed as they ventured honest answers while trying to maintain a respectable amount of spiritual dignity.

Shirley, a robust sin-dabbler, didn't squirm. She didn't even bat a blonde eyelash as she matter-of-factly informed us, "I can't answer the last three questions because my pencil broke." No interpreter was necessary; we all knew what she was saying.

Tidying up the usual postsession chaos, I chuckled while tossing Shirley's crumpled lesson leaflet into the trash.

In reflecting on her words, I was forced to admit that I had sometimes done that. When probed with piercing questions, I too have tried to pacify the Teacher with lame excuses. When His love has penetrated the private areas of the soul, I have yelled, "I can't answer that question, God; I broke my pencil."

At times He may smile, but He always offers another sharpened pencil and demands an up-front answer. He just stands there, waiting for an acceptable reply, and proceeds to make the necessary corrections.

Someday when the final exam is upon me, I will have a better chance at a passing score because He is my Teacher here—and He has an endless supply of sharpened pencils.

# Rest in Him

Sitting in my special corner in the wee morning hours today, I noticed the empty city buses regularly passing the window. Early Saturday travelers are rare, so bus after empty bus passed. The drivers were not anxious as they swept by. They weren't embarrassed because they were driving a busload of empty seats through Calgary's darkened streets.

Not a one of those navigators parked his bus outside our door to campaign for uninterested folk to get on board; they didn't go off their charted course to seek out passengers. They just kept right on driving their buses on their laid-out route.

While reading the ancient ancestry records from 1 Chronicles, my mind was more interested in the buses than the scores of unfamiliar names. I guess the Holy Spirit didn't feel those names were all that important for me that day either, because He stepped out of the shadows and began His gracious lesson.

"You know, you have been too concerned at times about people responding to the message. Instead of just doing the work I have cut out for your hands and staying right on the path, you have tried to entice people into the Kingdom. That is My job. The success or failure of your given task will not be measured by the response of others to you, but instead, by how well you have trusted My promises and obeyed My commands."

There was no argument. I have too often been set on *making* people see Christ's love, playing the role of His cheerleader and social secretary. I have gone off God's mapped-out route to beg folk to accept Christ's Gift.

Oh, Christians do want to see people genuinely won to the Kingdom. It would be wonderful if the entire world would

51

repent and be saved. But others will never make it simply because I have done the right things. They too will have to set their hearts and minds on Jesus Christ. We must continue to reach out in love but leave the work of conviction to the Holy Spirit.

Today it is my goal to be on course, to be in place, doing my job. If at the end of these hours there is a full bus, great! But if people refuse to accept the ride, there will be no shame, because I will still be on course.

## Ask for His Leading

"When he, the Spirit of truth is come, he will guide you" (John 16:13).

Yours truly is a whimpering, slushy, sympathetic idiot! You know, the kind that would forbid the surgeon to apply his scalpel, hoping to rescue the patient from pain, even though that pain would eventually bring healing.

Recently, dedicating himself to the task of lessening his work-laden mother's torture, Arron decided to help with the dinner dishes. His services had not been enlisted; he volunteered them. Reaching for a saucer to be baptized in the bubbly water, his chubby hands lost control. Crash! One less saucer to wash.

Not long ago Marion ran away from home. She claimed her life was miserable with her folks. Without consulting our Heavenly Father to see if my help was needed, I dashed in to save the day. Her life was nearly smashed beyond all hope of repair.

Sensitivity to the needs of others is a necessity if we are to serve Christ; yet this desire to impetuously intervene every time God dons His surgical gown has to be surrendered. Often He is operating in the lives of loved ones, even though we are unfamiliar with the procedure.

With His help, I am learning to let the Master Surgeon do His work and to assist only when He requests.

## Fill My Cup, Lord

Last night after Walter left to get the baby-sitter, I bowed in my special corner just to be near our Father for a few minutes, to ask for His love to genuinely flow through me to our friends.

He came; there was fullness.

This morning, while waiting for Him in the prayer spot, I was hungry. Oh, how I longed to be fed by the Living Bread. There was a craving to be satisfied by His Spirit, to be nourished to meet the challenges of this day.

If I had skipped the prayer feast in those wee hours, my spirit would not have starved to death; but oh, how weak and frail it would have been by the time Tabitha's disobedience called for loving patience beyond natural strength.

To keep this body running well, I eat regularly and seek to prepare well-balanced meals that will provide me with physical energy.

Yet a greater privilege is to come to the Master's table daily. We all need the spiritual food He prepares. He is waiting and calling, *"Come and dine"* (John 21:12).

# 5

## The Guiding, Reproving Spirit

# He Convicts Us of Sin

"And when he is come, he will reprove the world of sin, and of righteousness, and of judgment" (John 16:8).

Rick and Merle were showing me a coin trick after the evening worship service. Somehow they exchanged one quarter in my hands with another one; and I still don't have the maneuver figured out.

"How'd you do that?" I kept asking them. Shrugged shoulders and wicked grins were the only answers received.

Last night I dreamed some disgusting things. They were still on my mind while in the prayer corner this morning. It was hard to imagine why one should even dream such things; then somehow the Holy Spirit came and showed a need in my heart.

I sighed, "How'd You do that, Lord? How did You use an evil night thought to convict me of something I wasn't even aware of?" In amazement, my cleansed spirit sat in adoration of the ongoing work of the Holy Spirit.

Christ has the best in mind every time He reveals a flaw in our souls. If sin is a part of us, we cannot reflect the perfect love of Jesus Christ. Conviction needs to grip us when we are erring; and it does if we're spiritually alert.

How He does it is a mystery, but it's great!

# It Doesn't Pay to Disobey

"Behold, to obey is better than sacrifice, and to hearken than the fat of rams" (1 Sam. 15:22).

There he is again, seated on a hard, straight-backed dining room chair, nose in the corner. Jan has been in a corner more than he has been out lately. It seems all our children go through times of badness. This is Jan's week.

We have a phrase that is repeated for the one who has to spend time on the hot seat. The misdeed that caused him to be punished is discussed, then we try to help him understand that he never comes out on top when he goes against Daddy's or Mommy's wishes. We remind him: "It doesn't pay to disobey."

The lectures may not be doing the children much good. By every indication they don't, but the message is beginning to sink into *my* heart.

Disobedience only wastes our time and brings setbacks in our spiritual lives. God is a very conscientious Father. He will not tolerate our misbehavior any more than we will tolerate it in our children.

Last week, while trying to write a spiritual lesson that God was applying to my life, I decided to spruce up the story with just a wee lie. It wouldn't do any harm, and no one would know. It certainly was more sensational than the bare facts. Besides, the devotional was written to help build God's kingdom in my heart.

After finishing writing, I filed the paper away and forgot about it. But that night I was absolutely miserable. I had stretched the truth just enough to make it more interesting, but God had stuck my nose in the corner for doing it.

Finally I gave in. "OK, God, You win! I will tell the whole truth and nothing but the truth. But what does it matter anyway?"

His smile was soothing. "It doesn't pay to disobey," was His only reminder.

My words! He had used them to bring needed correction. I grinned at His message and rolled over for a bit of rest. He had forgiven. With His help that sin would be corrected in the morning.

# True Love Means Respect

"And whoso shall receive one such little child in my name receiveth me" (Matt. 18:5).

Walter and I were discussing the day as he helped with the dinner dishes. Arron stepped to the kitchen door and cautiously asked, "Are you excused from the table, Mommy?" He wanted to get a pencil, and knew he was not to interrupt us if we were still at the table.

"What do you think, Honey?" I responded, rather sarcastically.

He mumbled his "Yes" as he opened the closet door. And I knew I had failed.

I turned to him and confessed, "I am sorry for answering that way, Sweetie."

My little imp stood dumbfounded for a number of seconds before he asked, "Why are you, Mommy?"

"Because I didn't answer you very nicely," I began. "I don't think Jesus wants me to talk like that."

Arron hesitated before he impulsively hugged my leg. "I forgive you," he whispered. I knew he had. And I knew Jesus had come to our kitchen. Tears swelled in my eyes, and I returned my wee one's loving affection.

The Holy Spirit has continued to speak to me about the way I respond to the children's questions and comments. He has instructed me never to speak to them in a way I would not want to have someone speak to me.

They are just little, and maybe they could get used to having Mommy insinuate they are stupid by the tone of her voice; but Jesus would never speak to them in such a way.

As we listen, chat, and laugh with our children, they need to feel the worth of their lives. They need to know they are important to us and to God, that we respect them. They need to see Jesus in us.

59

Arron's shocked ears heard Jesus speak tonight. And he also knows we love him.

God knows I am thankful that He reminded me to speak politely always, even to our tiny tots.

## The Lord Disciplines Those He Loves

"He disciplines us for our good, that we may share his holiness" (Heb. 12:10, RSV).

Our children had to be disciplined yesterday. Not many days go by that they don't have to be corrected for some reason or other, but then it is soon forgotten.

Yesterday one of Layton's school friends came to call on him. Being involved in the middle of a pressing task when Tim interrupted, I told him Layton was not here.

Instead of accepting the answer, this budding lawyer was determined to know where Layton had gone and for what reason. It did not seem like it was any of his business. Finally, I blurted rather roughly: "He has gone with his daddy, and he will not be home in time to play."

Tim's shoulders drooped as he turned to go his way. His glance reflected the pain inflicted.

Immediately my heart jumped to my throat. I had failed to respond to this little guy in the pure love that God's Holy Spirit wanted to pour through my being. My soul was being disciplined for misbehavior.

Tim's crumpled face haunted me deep into the night. His saddened look followed as I pried myself from the cozy bed to pray this morning. Upon opening the Bible to study the Scriptures, my spirit was in dire need of healing. I cried, "Father, I am so sorry for hurting Tim. That was not like You at all. Please forgive."

Comfort came, and God's love flooded my soul as He spoke: "You were wrong to speak gruffly to that child. But I have punished you and have shed new grace in your heart. You are forgiven, and the deed is forgotten."

My soul was released from the guilt, and I resolved to move closer to the Cross. It is only in Christ's shadow that His love can reach the deepest reserves of the spirit. I do want to be like Him!

In disciplining our children, I pray that permanent corrections will be made in their characters. What a delight to know that our Heavenly Father corrects us and that His desired changes are being made in my disciplined heart.

## Needed: An Enlarged Heart

While my hands were drenched in sudsy water, the ladies curiously questioned what the next item on the agenda would be. Our New Year's Eve potluck dinner was just the beginning of the evening's celebration.

Caral, a faithful and positive witness, entered carrying another stack of grimy plates to be washed.

"Well," she offered with a laugh, "I could tell everyone my problems. That would take us up to midnight, I am sure."

Self-righteously I commented, "I could share all my blessings; that would take us up to *next* New Year's Eve."

That statement was true, because God had been warming my heart in a tremendous way. Yet as I stood scrubbing plate after dirty plate, the Holy Spirit stepped up close. By the way He approached, it was plain that I had failed to be like the Master.

His emphasis was clear. "Caral is hurting. You know she never complains. She was trying to let you know that something is bothering her."

Having been less than sensitive to this loyal soul, I couldn't finish the chores quickly enough. I had received a command from the Father and wanted to obey.

As soon as the dishwater slurped down the drain, the search was on for Caral. The two of us had a long chat. Her pain was genuine. I was sorry for not having heard her the first time she tried to share.

Every time my mouth blurts out crushing comments to a hurting world, it causes me sorrow. This shows such a lack of our Savior's likeness. The ears of the soul are often plugged with selfish interests.

Last year almost ended on a defeated note, simply because of being so wrapped up in personal joy that the sigh of a fellow Christian was not getting through.

May Christ enlarge our hearts. My greatest desire for the fresh year at hand is to be able to offer more and more love to the world.

## Perfect Love

"Bless them that curse you, do good to them that hate you . . . that ye may be the children of your Father which is in heaven" (Matt. 5:44-45).

This week we have been enjoying game nights with members of our church family. We have battled tops, checkered Chinese-style, and Flinched for three nights. It has been fun.

But it has also been a time of deep learning. Having always tried to be a warm hostess to everyone who enters our home, I never realized that the Holy Spirit considered this a part of one's ministry.

After one night's fellowship time, I was busying myself with the cleanup of dirty cups and saucers, feeling totally exhausted from many late nights and early mornings. But my Friend still felt it was a good time to chat. As He generously gave extra strength for the chores, He began: "Do you feel you were completely loving tonight?"

There was no need to hesitate. "No. But they were in such a rotten mood, there didn't seem to be any purpose in trying to pamper them out of it."

"But," the Comforter continued, "they were guests in your home."

"Yes, but it is so hard to be loving to them when they are so determined to be miserable. They don't respond to anything."

Christ stood silent. Finally He spoke: "I washed all of the disciples' feet . . . even Judas's."

My heart was torn. "O Jesus, I am sorry. I do want to be Your servant. Please forgive. Please take the shredded delights of this evening and turn them into something completely beautiful for You. You deserved a loving hostess to all of these guests. With Your help, I will never behave that way again but will serve others as You did . . . even them."

Though a weary body still craved a refreshing night's sleep, a newly cleansed spirit was already prepared to face the day ahead.

## Growing Pains

One week ago God convicted in a certain area.

As I sat in the special corner reading His Word, an Old Testament law jumped out of the pages. It gripped my heart until I felt almost choked.

Instead of immediately obeying this new insight, I tried to convince God that the command was only part of the old covenant. But He wasn't swayed by the rationalization.

As Tuesday's ironing was being completed, the lopsided debate continued. God offered no rebuttal. His Word had said it all. Some of my clothes were less modest than He wanted. So the decision was to make a deal with Him. "Now, God, here's my fleece. You ask this wealthy friend of ours in the States to send a check to replace these clothes with more appropriate ones, and that will prove it is Your will."

This morning, while plodding through the 10 chapters from the Bible, I figured my spirit was out of whack only because we had been up late last night, and because I had a cold.

I pleaded with Jesus to just let me sense His presence. He came but gently asked, "Are you ready to trust and obey? Or are you going to obey only if I work a miracle?"

I knew what He was talking about. My heart ached in realizing how near disaster this debate had come.

"O Jesus, I am sorry!" I cried. "I love You more than life itself. These things don't mean anything when considering how much You love me. Lord, I will obey and I will trust!"

His perfect peace was mine.

I do long to be Christ's lady, to be my best for Him. I want His genuine sweetness to flow through my spirit, so people can see Him. The inappropriate items of wearing apparel that He talked about may not be evil in themselves, yet they are not included in the Potter's image for my new life. It is thrilling to think He is not finished, and thanks can be given for His life-giving conviction. At this minute the Holy Spirit is pouring His perfect love into my heart.

## No Human Being Can Tame the Tongue

"Let the words of my mouth, and the meditation of my heart, be acceptable in thy sight, O Lord, my strength, and my redeemer" (Ps. 19:14).

The senior Gilroys are teeth nuts. Our children know that they are always expected to dash straight to the bathroom from the table to scrub away remaining food particles.

As they scoot from the kitchen, they are accustomed to hearing me call after them, "Clean them well, and don't forget to brush your tongue."

Our little ones are surely weary of hearing how clinging bacteria can jump from the tongue to the teeth and cause dreaded cavities.

It would be great if the filthy stuff that often corrodes the tongue could be cleansed as easily. All too often words that reveal decay and dirt slide from our mouths. The Holy Spirit helps us, but more of His purified sweetness needs to flow from our lips.

This morning as Walter and I discussed some upcoming events, we were on two separate wave lengths. Because we were not thinking together, the temptation came to spurt out impatient phrases that would have wounded my husband. Fortunately the thoughtless words were cleansed from my open mouth. What a glorious time we have had in each other's love this day.

It seems that the Holy Spirit must stand ready with His preventative brush constantly. Again today my mouth needed to be scrubbed. Some cruel, speculative thoughts were forming in my head and working their way to my tongue. Even though the facts were straight, the Holy Spirit was determined that they would not be vocalized. Those words were much better left unsaid.

The spiritual cavity-fighter has to be applied to my tongue many times throughout the waking hours; but that's all right. It would be better to have restraint put on the mouth than to have the soul rotted out by some insensitive thoughts rashly uttered.

In going about the tasks of this day, I can almost hear the Father call, "Don't forget to brush your tongue."

# Love One Another

"A new commandment I give unto you, That ye love one another, as I have loved you" (John 13:34).

Love has found our home a pretty difficult place to survive at times. Whenever selfish ambitions have interrupted the flow of love between Walt and me, a shadow of hatred and gloom has fallen across all of our lives.

One Sunday morning tension mounted between us. We had been discussing a distasteful matter that had developed in our relationship. Our voices got louder and louder as our words got crueler and crueler. We did not yell at each other (we were too sophisticated for that), but we certainly made ourselves heard!

Charity was cradled on her daddy's knee. She squirmed deeper and deeper into Walter's arms as she listened to us fight. She had never heard her mommy and daddy argue like this, and it frightened her.

Quietly she observed the combat scene until she could stand it no longer. With a loud cry she blurted, "Jesus is Boss!"

In those three little words, Charity brought us back. She did not know a scripture to quote us, but she certainly knew what had to be the truth. The Bible says, *A little child shall lead them* (Isa. 11:6). We knew more clearly just what God meant, because Charity had enough insight to realize her mommy and daddy were getting nowhere in their self-ishness, that Jesus had to be Boss. If not, love would be banned from our home . . . perhaps forever.

But love reentered our lives. Somewhere between those first casual comments and the last cutting remarks, we had cast it out; but love returned because of Charity's urgent reminder.

That scene took place some time ago. Walter and I had not

yet been baptized in the perfect love of the Holy Spirit, and we were in the process of demanding self-satisfying love from each other.

Jesus is Lord of our lives now! And even though we continue to have disagreements, the Holy Spirit is teaching us to work out our differences in "giving love" instead of "taking love."

## He Will Guide You

"Howbeit when he, the Spirit of truth, is come, he will guide you into all truth" (John 16:13).

Everyone had been excused from the breakfast table when Tabitha asked if she could blow out the candle. She huffed and puffed! After a few more frantic attempts she looked up, frustrated.

"Honey," I told her, "you are not blowing at the fire; you are just wasting your breath."

Charity had been observing her big sister's efforts and seriously added, "You don't want to waste *all* your breath!"

Laughter filled the kitchen as Tabitha finally got herself aimed in the right direction. She aimed one big gust at the candle—and swish! Victory was hers!

Trying to bring order to the after-meal chaos, I wondered just how often I too have blown and blown and blown, never succeeding because of not being aimed in the right direction.

Too many times we set out in our own strength and wisdom to pursue admirable goals. But we never get anywhere because we do not seek the Spirit's guidance. Instead, we can easily waste all our spiritual breath.

How about spending hours with a community group, writing newspaper articles for them, only to realize we are not blowing in the right direction. This is not doing anything wrong but is using our talents to accomplish worldly purposes.

Many of us spend days reading choice novels, which in themselves are not evil. At the close of those days, however, we are not any nearer eternal goals than in the morning.

Foolishly we watch too much television, generally careful to tune out the violent and vulgar programs, but losing ourselves in its pretense. Then we discover ourselves sluggishly facing the next day because of not having exercised any spiritual energy during those hours.

With Jesus as Guide, let us not waste the breath graciously given for this day. Tonight, victory can be ours!

## Caution

"Watch and pray, that ye enter not into temptation" (Matt. 26:41).

Last night's secret pal Christmas party must have been smiled upon by heaven. Not only was Shirley's Christmas cactus in full bloom, but the world was carpeted by pure, white snowflakes. It was easy to feel festive, even at this early date.

Driving to our hostess's country home, Marg and I admired the snow with childlike enthusiasm. Every glistening flake landed perfectly. Calgary was picture-postcard magnificent.

Yet our praise for the white crystals was not flawless. The limited visibility and slippery pavement made travel treacherous. We had to admit it presented a problem. We definitely had no desire to spend the gala evening in a ditch.

The Holy Spirit has gently been removing scales from my eyes of late. Many beautiful highways must be cautiously approached. So many things are delightful. They make the world sparkle, and yet they can present a road hazard for the soul.

My life has been blessed by cherished relationships. Dearest comrades bring happiness, acceptance, and satisfaction. But those friends can cause me to slide off the road if frequent late-night fellowships make early morning prayer and Bible time hazy and difficult.

The antiques decorating our home are a delight. Their presence surrounds us with the beauty our souls crave. They remind us of the charm of previous years and even stir thanksgiving for modern-day gadgets. Yet if the preservation of these artifacts becomes more precious than the joy of the healthy, carefree children sharing this house, we will be slipping from the way.

Even the tasty, healthful bounty which supplies us with physical energy can send us crashing if indulged in beyond what the body needs.

God intends for us to thoroughly enjoy all the blessings He has sent. But should they begin to obstruct spiritual vision, our lifetimes could be wasted in a ditch.

Marg and I did not slip and slide over the road dangerously last night. Her adept driving met the challenge the heavy snowfall offered. May the journey through the hours of this beautiful day be as successfully made.

# 6
## The Compassionate Spirit

# They Cannot Be Good Without God

"Moreover as for me, God forbid that I should sin against the Lord in ceasing to pray for you: but I will teach you the good and the right way" (1 Sam. 12:23).

Very possibly Mr. Feeney, the principal, would be willing to come down here and pack all our belongings if we should decide to move. With four representatives from the Gilroy household attending his school, he certainly has his hands full.

The first bit of news we received today as the kids came home for lunch was that Jan had pulled the firebell switch. We could imagine the chaos. No one knew there was to be a drill, so kids went scurrying everywhere. The youthful principal spanked our lad soundly, and we warned Jan against ever *even thinking* about touching that lever again.

After the kids were excused from the table, Walter and I enjoyed a good laugh over the comical description we had received; yet, while cleaning up lunchtime crumbs, I seriously reflected on the incident.

Our prayer for Jan and for all our charges is that God will keep their hands from touching sin. There is so much in the world to entice them, and temptations have already threatened their little souls.

"Jesus," my heart sighed, "You know the delightful lures between here and the school. You know that the greenhouse windows make perfect targets, and that in the store, coveted felt markers are always on display. Please, Lord, shout 'No' in the ears of our tots as they are tempted to follow the urgent desires in their hearts. Don't let evil wreck their lives."

Our children love us and want to please us. But when they are out of our presence, they cannot face the wiles of the devil without extra help. They are too little to always stand firm against the pulls toward sin; they cannot be good without God.

I am praying that Tabitha, Jan, Layton, Arron, and even Charity will invite Jesus into their hearts during this year. Even though they are so very young, they have been tempted to do wrong. At times they have yielded to those temptations. Therefore our little ones need the Savior.

# A Prayer for People

*"Thy kingdom come. Thy will be done in earth, as it is in heaven" (Matt. 6:10).*

This afternoon, instead of touching our toes, our exercise group will spend its time stuffing treat bags for our Sunday School children. Perhaps this exercise will prove more profitable than physical exertion.

As we put assorted goodies into each little sack, hearts will be praying for our Sunday School pupils. Many of them come to our services without their parents. They get out of bed, fix their breakfast, and meet the bus on their own. They long to be with us and to learn about the Christ child.

Lord Jesus, You love these children more than we do. You are very aware of their unhappy homelives; of the frequent beatings some of them receive; of the neglect they must endure.

Please let these wee spirits sense Your presence through these treats provided for them. As they reach into these bags, may they pull out more than chocolates and gumdrops. Place Your love inside each bag. Please open these children's eyes to Your miracles this Christmas. Bend down to their souls and whisper to their hearts the true meaning of Your birth.

And Savior, we would not ask for the little ones alone; we plead for their parents as well. As they come into Your house Sunday evening to listen to their children's recitations, may their hearts be strangely warmed. Tug at their consciences. Sit with them in those pews that have been dedicated to Your gospel—and reveal yourself to them. These miracles we humbly ask in Your blessed name. Amen.

## Through the Eyes of the Spirit

"I pray also that the eyes of your heart may be enlightened" (Eph. 1:18, NIV).

Jan is one of the sweetest little Indian boys we have ever seen. When we take the children out for a day, Jan is usually the one whom people notice first: partly because he is so adorable, and partly because he is so Indian. When people admire our miniature brave, they notice his gigantic brown eyes, his poker-straight black hair, his high cheekbones.

Yet that is just part of our little fella. When looking at his smile, I can also see his great love for nature: his rock collection, the scores of wildflower bouquets he has gathered, and the delight he discovers when watching a springtime ladybug. Our little Indian boy may be a future botanist or an artist who could bring more beauty to this world.

As his mother, I see, more than Jan's perfectly tinted face, the potential hidden within him.

Since my heart has been freed from the fettering desire to worship myself, the Holy Spirit is teaching me more and more to see all mankind as He sees: not for what they are, but for what they can become when transformed by the healing blood of Jesus Christ.

So far, my eyes have just begun to be opened to more than the outward appearance. When the drunken neighbor came to our door for a chat, it was hard to see the potential beauty God planted deep within him, but it was necessary to see it. When the ill-clad man begged for some warm coffee, it was hard to see the gleam lighting his tired eyes; but it was there, and I caught a bit of it. When some of the teens in my Sunday School class behave foolishly, it is difficult to see the maturity their souls can reach once they have been transformed by the love of the Savior and by the power of His Holy Spirit.

How much better it is to see more than alcohol-drowned eyes, sloppy clothes, and immature teens. More profitable is it to see the glory buried deep in the soul of every person.

It will take still more of the grace of God in order to see one's fellowman clearly. But the good news is that this grace also is available through walking with the Holy Spirit.

# 7
# The Spirit
# of Power

# Power to Train Them

"Train up a child in the way he should go: and when he is old, he will not depart from it" (Prov. 22:6).

. Jan and Arron's caseworker came for a visit this week to discuss our foster children's future.

The boys' father loves them. He wants them back with him. He has never abused them, yet his love has been irresponsible.

When their dad felt like feeding his two charges, they ate well. But when caring for their physical needs did not fit his mood, the boys were left nearly to starve until he felt like being a father again.

Our continuous prayer these days is that God will guide the social services as they decide the fate of our boys. We crave the best for them.

A practicing parent can understand this young father's frustration.

There have been times when I would rather not be bothered by supplying our children with their emotional and physical needs. Who does not want more time to pursue his own desires? Yet because of love for them, I push immediate preferences aside.

Often it would be more convenient to let our tribe do as they please. Yet this kind of inconsistent disciplining would destroy them. Time must be taken to correct them and to guide their little lives. *I must be their mother every minute of every day.*

There have been times when I have been buried deep in daydreams and creative moods. At these moments, their bursts of spontaneous affection have seemed almost like intrusions. But if the door is always to remain ajar between us, I must receive my wee ones' impetuous lovin's with open arms.

Every day it is obvious I am not big enough for this job. My patience cannot stretch far enough. Inerrant wisdom to see where this day's activities may lead them is not always appropriated. Who is smart enough to answer all their questions? Help is needed.

Thank God, that help is available. The Holy Spirit loves our children, and He loves us. He does provide what is needed for all of us on a daily basis.

Walter and I are committed to be mature, consistent, loving parents. We are ever praying that our children's futures will be brighter because they have been members of our family.

## No

"Resist the devil, and he will flee from you" (James 4:7).

Our children have always remained sweet in spite of the fun teasing they get from their daddy. Today lunchtime dessert had been served. Just as Charity started to tackle hers, Walter stuck his fork into it and joked, "Charity doesn't want hers, so I think I'll eat it."

Accustomed to his behavior, she immediately responded, "Uh, uh!" and that was that.

Slowly I am learning to respond that quickly to the devil when he comes around to tempt. Often he suggests, "Hey, look what you could get out in the world," but I draw back into the Savior's arms.

Then he sneaks up and whispers, "Who would notice if you just left that job for today? You could do it tomorrow."

The answer comes a bit more hesitantly this time, but it

does come. "No! My tasks for this day must be completed. I am sure God will have plenty for me to do tomorrow."

And when one feels mistreated, Satan snarls, "Are you going to let her get by with that? It is time to stand up and demand your rights." For a brief second there is temptation to give in; but looking into the face of Jesus, I crave His likeness and refuse the temptation.

Times come when I am not ready with a firm "Uh, uh!" After having yielded to the tempter's bidding, my heart is broken. That day's dessert has been missed out on because of a refusal to stand firm.

Charity enjoys the games her daddy plays with her, even if he does keep her on her toes. But the devil's tactics are not made to entertain. Approval of his suggestions will lose victory for the soul. One must be on guard and respond always with a quick "Uh, uh!"

Today I am prepared for Satan, for he will come. That is his job, and he does it too well. But time spent in the presence of the Conqueror will then not permit the devil to snatch the joy from life.

## "Let All . . . Anger . . . Be Put Away from You"
### (Eph. 4:31)

"You are the world's seasoning, to make it tolerable. If you lose your flavor, what will happen to the world? And you yourselves will be thrown out and trampled underfoot as worthless" (Matt. 5:13, TLB).

A salt-free diet would probably destroy many of us, even though we try to limit the amount we eat. We think we would perish without it!

Any kitchen-oriented woman realizes that this seasoning

81

substance must be added to the vegetables before they begin to boil. Otherwise, the white crystals will not properly spread their zesty flavor into the food. If salt is not added early in the cooking process, prepared dishes can be ruined.

My culinary skills leave much to be desired, but I am trying to develop them in order to please the family's taste buds more and more.

The Holy Spirit has been trying to improve my temper skills since He cleansed my heart. The results of His love being applied to my spirit have been miraculous. It is hard to believe that His grace permeates the soul so naturally.

There was a time I doubted this was possible. Even though desperately longing to be like Jesus, I knew what bitter ingredients filled my wretched heart. But now, since His love is present before the crisis comes, His grace is being found sufficient.

Yet there are times when the boiling starts, when it's questionable that I will be the savory Christian He wants to create by the growth of my sanctified spirit. And then, much to my delighted surprise, there He stands, shaker in hand, pouring His seasoning into my open soul; and rich taste enters my being.

One learns to ask Him to shake His patient compassion into the heart early in the irritation's cooking stage so that the soul will always reflect His sweet Spirit.

The Lord's sanctifying touch leaves nothing to be desired —except a greater craving to be full of His pure love. He generously pours His grace into the soul of His receptive children.

## The Steadying Hand

What a time Layton had learning to balance that bicycle. As we ran along beside him, holding the two-wheeler steady, he would grip the handlebars so tightly that the front end wobbled. And we also had to keep a firm grip.

Slowly but surely we were able to lessen our grasp, until finally he was confident enough to pedal around the parking lot with us just trotting by his side. Then he took off . . . Crash! That was one way of stopping.

Certain thoughts about these past few months since my heart's cleansing come to the surface.

Oh, there is a longing to learn to be steady, to never grovel in self-pity and self-centeredness; but that can be possible only if Christ's power holds one firmly. May I never grow independent of the One balancing the soul.

There is a desire to learn to freely glide in the love filling my heart, but it must be ever flowing from the Holy Spirit.

To pedal the road of usefulness is a top priority, but only His transforming touch can make me worth anything.

Oh, I am determined to ride this bike of faith, but the ride will never be successful without the Lord running alongside.

Layton was right to seek independence from us, but we need the hand of God to steady our souls—always. And He does.

# 8

# Spirit-anointed Service

# He Affirms My Ministry

"Now there are diversities of gifts, but the same Spirit" (1 Cor. 12:4).

Tabitha held out an itsy-bitsy Cheerio on her spoon. "I'm going to eat this baby Cheerio," she told us with an impish smile.

After she swallowed her prey, I teased, "Did he cry when you bit him?"

With a shake of the head, she instantly replied, "No, he knows he's a Cheerio."

He was created to be eaten. And I was created to be a wife and a mother.

Sometimes, because of enthusiastically wanting to see the church increase, I have laid that calling to one side. I have tried to fulfill my husband's calling or to do the work of other officers in the church; but I was created to be a wife and a mother.

Sometimes, because of having varied interests, I have been tempted to fly from this nest to pursue them; but I was created to be a wife and a mother.

This calling can be fulfilled only through the blood of Jesus Christ cleansing and enriching the spirit through faithfulness to duty.

When one of our wee ones dashes into my arms, sobbing with penitent tears, it is crystal-clear that God knows best.

When a soul comes into a closer relationship to Jesus Christ, the pastor's wife too receives the joy of the angels in heaven because of having prayerfully supported her pastor-husband.

In this calling one is not limited. No boundaries bar me

from breaking all records as a dedicated, loving wife and mother; and I long to be the lady God created me to be.

So as the world around is going its exciting way, I am not being gobbled up by the family. Instead, I *know* and give thanks I was created to be a wife and a mother.

## We Can't Do It Alone

He was a retired Baptist minister, a dinner guest in our home. In preparing for his coming, I prayed that we might be a blessing to him.

We will never know if our efforts to welcome and love Mr. Easter were truly a blessing to him; but there is no doubt that his visit enriched our lives. His gentle spirit portrayed the Savior he has spent most of his lifetime serving.

Before he returned to his apartment, Mr. Easter asked if he could have a word of prayer with Walter and me. The four of us—for surely the Lord was in our midst—bowed our heads, and he opened his heart on our behalf. As he approached God for our guidance in raising the children, he whispered, "For they are not big enough or good enough to do this job without You."

The Amens were said, hands were shaken, farewells were made, and he departed. But the echoes of that sincere request for our home will ring in our hearts through the years.

His simple prayer request once again was a reminder of the awesomeness of our task. Again we realized how we need to be gripped by pure motives as we discipline, love, care for, and guide our children.

God's blessings have fallen on our home. We are undeserving, yet we enjoy everything that love can bring to a family. I have renewed the promise to ever seek God's design in the development of our charges. I face the job humbly, certain that this retired saint was right: We are not big enough or good enough.

We have one deep desire for the cluster of childish energy in our home. Before their years have been buried in sin, we pray that they will surrender their hearts to Christ. Walt and I alone cannot lead them to this faith. We must have wisdom and patience and love enough to plant the right seeds in their soul, all of which must come from above.

Our friend's glowing testimony and caring benediction has worked a miracle. The Lord of our home has been resurrected in my heart.

## Be Ye Also Ready

I had called the girls to get dressed for Sunday School. From the bathroom, I heard Tabitha reason with her little sister. "The clothes aren't laid out yet, but I am going to take off my pajamas so I'll be ready to put on my Sunday School dress when Mommy comes."

Charity agreed this was a good idea, and she began to prepare herself for her pretty church dress too.

As I entered the room, both girls were beaming. They had made every effort to be ready for me. They were delighted that I arrived so quickly so they could show me how good they were.

As I dressed them, tugging on bright white socks and fastening black patent shoes, I was pleased. The girls scurried back to their play, and I finished picking up odds and ends.

While hanging a pair of p.j. bottoms on the peg, I smiled. "O Jesus, I will be ready too, because of Your Holy Spirit in me. When You come, I will be clean and waiting for the bridal gown You prepared for Your Church."

God hasn't laid out our eternal apparel as yet. But for the time left to spend on this earth, I will be given opportunity to prepare for wearing it. May my soul be spotless when He comes. That is why it is vital to come to His fountain daily.

That is why it is important to make a new sacrifice of this life every morning.

When Christ comes, I want to be ready, having completed every bit of work He has given to do. I want our children to be fed and happy, the Sunday School lesson read, Walt's shirts ironed, the furniture dusted, and the dishes put away. I want to have encouraged the soul whom the Holy Spirit has laid on my heart.

It was delightful to hear Tabitha reasoning so well this morning, not just because it made preparing them for Sunday School easier, but also because she wanted to please me.

Our Father is worthy of pleasing, too. The Holy Spirit helps us be ready to receive our returning Lord.

# 9
# Our First Christmas in the Spirit

# "Be Ye Thankful"

"Let the peace of God rule in your hearts ... and be ye thankful" (Col. 3:15).

The note read: "To Mommy and Daddy. Thank you for everthing you give us." The spelling wasn't perfect, but the sincerity behind that spontaneous love letter was full.

Our little ones, caught up with the spirit of the quickly approaching holiday, spent the afternoon making gifts and hiding them for us to find. This note, tenderly wrapped in a homemade envelope, was tucked under some magazines in our room. Walter and I gave each of the kids a special I-love-you hug before we resumed our previous activities.

Reflecting on their heartfelt thankfulness, my soul swells with pride. It is so good that our children realized how fortunate they are, and that they are learning to express gratitude for *everything*.

I too must say, "Thank You." Oh, there is so much to be thankful for at this special time of the year.

How thankful I am for the wondrous presence of the Holy Spirit in my life. Also for Walter and the children. Again, a loving congregation and the nice, warm home they provide for our family are blessings. All this and more are causes for thankfulness.

But the victory over a temptation faced this morning is a reason for thanks. The Holy Spirit helped me to reject its call to a rotten attitude. God is doing something within me that was never dreamed possible.

That there was strength when the longed-for letter didn't come made for gratefulness. Loving patience is needed, the kind that will not slide into bitterness should someone neglect to pay attention to me.

I am thankful Layton was so silly when pulling on his snowsuit this afternoon. A thousand times a day I need to be reminded that he is just a child.

Our lives are full with every tangible thing needed to make us happy. But far superior to these material blessings are the spiritual gifts the Lord continues to send our way.

Our children overwhelmed me with their delightful game this morning. They even taught a Christmas lesson through it. "Thank You" must be said to our Father for everything He gives.

## When He Is Come

"This is the nicest Christmas we've ever had!" Tabitha exclaimed as we ate our buttered rolls in the warmed-up car.

We were resting from our trek up the mountainside. We had trudged through layers of snow to cut our mighty Christmas pine, and our fingers and toes were still tingly from the frosty hike. The rolls, hot coffee, juice, and doughnuts that Grandma sent us tasted yummy after the steep climb.

The entire outing had been blessed by God. A bright, Alberta sun smiled on us the entire day, and we all felt like rejoicing. Charity continued to chant, "God is so good," while the other children sang their favorite carols with Daddy and Mommy.

In our hearts, we are certain this *is* the nicest Christmas we have ever had. There haven't been any changes in our traditional preparations for the holiday. We have searched for Dougie the Elf as usual; we have opened the tiny Advent calendar windows as usual; we have cut and pasted our additions to the Yule collage as usual; yet this is not a usual Christmas.

If we asked the kids what the change has been, they would not be able to express it. But it is easy to see they know something is different. Today as they chattered and romped in the knee-deep snow, once again my heart praised God for a released, sanctified spirit.

Because of this glorious freedom, I am at liberty to slide down the mountainside and giggle with Charity, to listen to Layton's corny jokes and roar with laughter, to patiently answer Tabitha's continuous questions, and to wrap Arron and Jan in motherly warmth.

Who can explain the change? Who needs to? The Gilroys are having the nicest Christmas ever!

## My Prayer of Thanks

The kids and I had to eat our day-before-Christmas breakfast without Daddy this morning. He is sick. While preparing the meal, I was disappointed that the day's plans were going to have to be altered. I asked our Heavenly Father to please touch Walter's body if it would not interrupt any great plan. No one enjoys Christmas more than my husband.

Munching on cinnamon toast, the kids and I discussed the live Nativity scene we had gone to see last night. They were all enchanted by the sheep and donkey. Tabitha was glad the innkeeper had been just pretending to be mean when he told Joseph there wasn't any room for them in the little inn.

Layton was silent as the others chattered. Finally he observed, "Even though they had to sleep in a barn, they were thankful." His little eyes had caught the expressions of gratitude Mary and Joseph had made to the impatient innkeeper as he led them to the barn.

My soul instantly responded, "O Jesus, I am thankful too, even though Walter is not well enough to participate in this very special day with us.

"Walt adds so much to our Christmas that he is desperately missed when he is absent. I can still see him quietly enjoying the Christmas tree last night with Tabitha on his knee. Together they captured a meaningful seasonal moment.

"And his voice chiming, 'Two more days 'til Christmas! Two more days 'til Christmas!' still rings through the house today. I am thankful for the spirit he displays for all of us, and that he loves us so much that we don't seem complete without him near.

"Lord, even though Walter is not well, and it looks as if our Christmas will be a bit less than what we had anticipated, I am thankful for all he means to us. Thank You for this Christmas lesson.

"And thank You for Layton, who listened with his heart to the message of Your birth. Amen."

## Thoughts for a New Year

"He [chastens us] for our profit, that we might be partakers of his holiness" (Heb. 12:10).

Typing is not one of my greatest skills. Probably before this page is completed, there will be enough mistakes made to send my 11th grade commercial teacher to an early grave. We all try to make as few errors as possible; it is better that way. But when clumsy fingers tap the wrong letters, we will correct the mistakes immediately. Blemishes are noticeable, but corrections will be made.

Today I have been granted a brand-new spotless year to enjoy, and am determined to guard this sparkling, clean page. Certainly there will be mistakes and strikeovers before the days are lived out. But it is also certain that this year will be victorious because the blessed Holy Spirit is now shaping my hours and weeks and months. How could it be anything but glorious?

Even though many erased areas will be evident by the time next year comes around, no doubt God's best will be mine because of the decision to let Him lead. I have vowed to greet the Holy Spirit before the world awakes, asking His direction for every new day. As He types out His perfect image on my newly cleansed spirit, I will be obedient to His voice.

It is always easier to type flawlessly when we are absolutely certain of what we are going to type, when we have a definite plan in mind. I know which way is best to go this year. There is no decision to be made as to whether to have God's mind or that of the world. His perfection is possible; and its attainment will be within reach, because of the decision to follow Him. With the guidance and molding of the Holy Spirit applied to my soul, this year will be less marred than the one that preceded.

And I said to the man who stood at the gate of the year, "Give me a light that I may tread safely into the unknown."

And He replied, "Go out into the darkness and put your hand into the hand of God. That shall be to you better than light and safer than a known way."

—M. LOUISE HASKINS

# 10

## I Praise and Adore Him

# In Remembrance of Me
## (Luke 22:19)

Can you imagine? Surrounded by scores of shoppers, I stood bawling like a baby. I hadn't given much thought to November 11, Remembrance Day in Canada, and so wasn't prepared to deal with it in our hustly, bustly, sophisticated mall.

But there they were, those cute little Brownies and Cubs and the Bagpipe Corps trouping along, toting their wreaths and flags. The traditional 11 A.M. time of quiet reflection was upon us.

The musicians played some unfamiliar tune; our five imps gazed in wonder; some nearby adolescents smothered their giggles; and then it happened. Christ stepped out of the crowd, put His crucified arm around my shoulder, and I remembered: One Perfect Soul was unmercifully tortured, committing himself to our redemption.

Just as though my Friend had flashed them a cue, the bagpipers began to softly play, "Amazing grace, how sweet the sound . . ." There was no way to conceal the tears that splashed all over the place. One of the Brownie leaders warmed me with a smile, then her own eyes filled to overflowing. A reverent hush swept the frivolous throng, and spontaneously we worshiped.

My heart is moved with humble thanksgiving for the freedom we enjoy in this country. The grandest delight would be to tuck a personal thank-you note into the uniform of every man and woman who helped purchase it.

And the profoundest gratitude cannot express the joy bubbling in my soul because of the glorious freedom experienced daily. No power on earth can threaten the peace that He has brought, and continues to bring, today, tomorrow, and eternally. Looking into the Savior's eyes, my soul can simply whisper, "I love You."

It is good to remember—even when surrounded by scores of shoppers.

## Praise Him! Praise Him!

"I will bless the Lord at all times: his praise shall continually be in my mouth" (Ps. 34:1).

God has given me a very thoughtful secret prayer partner this year. Last night after the evening worship service, a brown paper bag was waiting for me at the back of the church. In that bag were several little slips of paper with spiritual promises for the new year written on them. Each promise is wrapped around a tiny gift of love.

I have been blessed so much by the two notes already opened that my heart cried out to thank the giver. It is frustrating to be bursting with joy and not to be able to show gratitude to the one who has created it. I want to thank my secret prayer partner. It would be fun to call her on the phone and tell her what her kind deed has meant, but I must wait until I am certain of her identity.

Moments of even deeper frustration were often mine during the darkest hours of my Christian life. This was due to trying so hard to stand on my own two feet, trying to convince myself that I didn't need the help of God. Even though doubting God's love, I sensed that He had to be the One bringing happiness to my life when it came. Even when desperately longing to turn my soul loose in praise, I was reluctant to do so. A cloud of gloomy unbelief hung over those days.

Compassionately Christ revealed himself once again, and

this time in such a way that I will never doubt His reality. He is the Giver of all good things, and my heart swells with songs of thanksgiving to Him. Spontaneously my soul bursts forth in praise to our blessed Redeemer for the unbelievable rapture flooding this soul.

# Security

"Who shall separate us from the love of Christ?" (Rom. 8:35).

This evening time is my favorite hour of the day.

Seeing our five little ones scrubbed, fed, and snuggled close to their daddy gives an immeasurable motherly delight. My heart sings glorious songs of thanksgiving that we are able to provide such love and warmth for these children.

Listening to them giggle and asking questions about the story Walter is reading to them, I move in just a bit closer to our Heavenly Father.

"I love You, Father," my heart swells. And He never fails to respond with love beyond description.

I can't doubt God's love anymore. He loves me far more than it is possible to imagine, and the feeling is mutual. He wants to provide life's best, and I want to be obedient. He wants me to be His child forever, and I rest in the peace that this assurance brings to my soul.

There have been times of struggle, times when I felt it necessary to toil and fret to remain in God's family.

But the more I snuggle close to our Father, the more I realize He will keep me as we keep our children. He longs to guide and discipline, and I long to trust and obey.

Now I am free to enjoy the love I have found, resting securely in His everlasting arms.